Young Heroes

Elizabeth Bloomer

Child Labor Activist

Jennifer Reed

KIDHAVEN PRESS

An imprint of Thomson Gale, a part of The Thomson Corporation

THOMSON

GALE

Detroit • New York • San Francisco • New Haven, Conn. • Waterville, Maine • London

THOMSON

—✳—™

GALE

LIBRARY OF CONGRESS CATALOGING-IN-PUBLICATION DATA

Reed, Jennifer.
    Elizabeth Bloomer : child labor activist / by Jennifer Reed.
    p. cm. — (Young heroes)
    Includes bibliographical references and index.
    ISBN 13: 978-0-7377-3615-1 (hardcover : alk. paper)
    ISBN 10: 0-7377-3615-1 (hardcover : alk. paper)
  1. Bloomer, Elizabeth, 1985– 2. Child labor—Juvenile literature. 3. Children's rights—Juvenile literature. 4. Social reformers—United States—Biography—Juvenile literature. I. Title. II. Title: Child labor activist.
  HD6231.R44 2006
  331.3'1092—dc22
[B]

                    2006018757

Contents

Chapter One

Just a Regular Kid

When she was twelve years old, Elizabeth Bloomer was like any other girl her age. She enjoyed school, sports, and spending time with her friends. She also was close to her parents, five sisters, and brother. As Elizabeth grew up, her family did many things together. She says, "We ate dinner together every night, at a set table with a candle lit in the center. We dressed up and attended **Mass** as a family every Sunday morning. And, we went to as many games and events of each other as we could." [1]

Elizabeth's life changed in 1997 when she joined a group of concerned students at Broad Meadows Middle School. Through the group she learned about Iqbal Masih, a young boy from Pakistan who had visited the school in 1994. Iqbal told the students about his life. His parents had sold him into slavery when he was only four years old. He was chained to a floor and forced to work at a loom in a carpet factory.

For Iqbal, there was no time for school or play. Iqbal was later freed and became an **advocate** for millions of other Pakistani children who were forced to work just as he had been.

The more Elizabeth learned about Iqbal and other children sold into slavery, the more disturbed she became. It was hard for her to imagine that children all over the world were forced to work. She decided to do whatever she could to help. Today she is one of America's leading **activists** against **child labor** abuses.

Elizabeth Bloomer (right), pictured with her sister Julie, credits her family as her inspiration.

Life in Quincy

Elizabeth Bloomer was born in Boston, Massachusetts, on June 23, 1985. Her father, William, is an assistant principal at a local elementary school. Her mother, Roberta, is a homemaker and is employed part-time by the Massachusetts Department of Education. She also does volunteer work in her church and community. Both of Elizabeth's parents attended Boston College. After they married, they decided to settle in the nearby suburb of Quincy. Elizabeth was their first child.

As a young girl, Elizabeth excelled at school, especially in her favorite subjects, reading and social stud-

Elizabeth's parents have always encouraged her and her siblings to work hard and help others.

ies. She was athletic, too. She started playing soccer when she was just six years old. Later, she enjoyed basketball, volleyball, and softball as well.

Strong Family Values

Elizabeth's parents encouraged her and her siblings to take part in sports, music, and other activities. They set only one rule—if the Bloomer children said they were going to do something, they had to stick with it. They could choose the activities they wanted to participate in, but the family rule held strong. "Once they are involved in something, we don't let them quit,"[2] says Roberta Bloomer.

Elizabeth's parents also urged their children to aid others in need. Elizabeth recalls that she and her family took part in many canned-food drives, can and bottle drives, and coat drives to assist Quincy's less fortunate families.

Elizabeth's parents passed on many other lessons, too. From her father, she learned the value of hard work and self-confidence. He taught Elizabeth early on that if she believed in herself, she could do anything she set her mind to do.

From her mother, Elizabeth learned to have a strong faith in God and to think of others before herself. Elizabeth says her mother is always supportive of her children and generous to people. For example, on Mother's Day, Roberta Bloomer buys her children presents because she says she would not be a mother without her kids.

Learning from Her Family

Elizabeth is close to her sisters and brother as well as her parents. As the oldest child, she often felt she needed to look out for her siblings. She enjoyed playing games with them, especially Wiffle ball in the backyard.

Elizabeth says that each of her siblings has taught her something unique. Mary, for example, has taught Elizabeth how to interact with people and encouraged her not to take life too seriously. Just a year and a half younger than Elizabeth, Mary was her first friend and playmate.

Elizabeth feels she is most like Laura, who is three years younger than she. Laura can finish Elizabeth's sentences, and the two find the same things funny. Laura has taught Elizabeth how to enjoy life and re-main a kid at heart.

Kristen, five years younger than Elizabeth, is a lot like their mother because she thinks about everyone but herself. At camp one time, Kristen decided to befriend a girl who was constantly being picked on. Kristen's gift, according to Elizabeth, is **compassion** and a genuine concern for others. Kristen has been a powerful exam-ple in Elizabeth's life.

Thomas, seven years younger than Elizabeth and the only boy in the family, is full of energy. Thomas pro-tects and takes care of his younger sisters. He has taught Elizabeth to stand up for herself and to do what she believes in, even if she has to do it alone.

Julie, ten years younger than Elizabeth, was diag-nosed with diabetes at the age of seven. Diabetes is an

Big smiles fill this portrait of the Bloomer sisters, (from left to right) Mary, Kristen, Elizabeth, Julie, Laura, and (in front) Caroline.

illness in which the body does not make enough insulin. Insulin is a substance that is needed to help sugar enter the body's cells, where it is used to make energy. Because she has diabetes, Julie must wear a pump that injects insulin into her stomach through a small tube. She has to prick her finger up to six times a day to check the level of sugar in her blood, and must be careful about what she eats. Julie has taught Elizabeth how to live for the moment and to be grateful for her life.

Caroline is the baby of the Bloomer family. She is fourteen and a half years younger than Elizabeth. She is happiest when she is playing games or simply spending

Elizabeth's sister, Caroline, and brother, Thomas, have helped her to appreciate the simple things in life.

time with the family. Caroline takes joy in small pleasures like throwing rocks into a puddle. She appreciates each small act of kindness, whether it is a hug, a smile, or a few hours of time spent with a beloved family member. From Caroline, Elizabeth has learned to enjoy the simple things in life, and she tries to do so each day.

Elizabeth's family has helped define who she is. She feels these lessons have made her a better and stronger person. "I wouldn't be Elizabeth Bloomer without my family, so any introduction that didn't include them, wouldn't really tell anything about me at all,"[3] she says.

Chapter Two

"A Bullet Can't Kill a Dream"

Elizabeth Bloomer attended private school from kindergarten through sixth grade. When she began seventh grade in 1997, however, she entered a public school, Broad Meadows Middle School. She made the change because the public school offered more activities that she wanted to be involved in. Elizabeth immediately joined the cross-country track team.

Something else caught her attention, too. School announcements often mentioned Iqbal meetings. Elizabeth says: "I had no idea what an 'Iqbal' meeting meant. So curiosity got the best of me and I decided to go to a meeting and see what it was all about. . . . I was fascinated with their energy. In the next couple of weeks, I saw clips of Iqbal's visit, news broadcasts, and the efforts of the Broad Meadows students. It was eye-opening and inspiring." [4]

At one Iqbal meeting, author and photographer Dr. David Parker shared his photographs of children in slavery. Most of the children pictured were from Southeast Asia. This meeting was a turning point for Elizabeth. She explains:

> The photos he was able to get (a dangerous task) were so **graphic** and moving. I was crying, as well as half the audience. That really did it for me. You can't see pictures like that and do nothing. We met with Dr. David Parker (and have since worked with him and been in contact) and discussed the pictures. From that time on, I knew I needed to take action.[5]

Child Labor

Parker's pictures showed children who worked in slavery instead of going to school or playing. Such child labor occurs in many countries around the world. Children are sold into slavery by their parents or kidnapped to work. The International Labor Organization believes that 246 million children between the ages of five and seventeen work in conditions that are often illegal, dangerous, or **exploitive.** They perform many different jobs such as weaving carpets in India, Pakistan, and Egypt and sewing clothes in Bangladesh. They mine for gold, diamonds, or coal in Colombia, Brazil, and El Salvador and fish or pick fruits and vegetables in Ecuador and the United States. Children even work as drug dealers and soldiers. They earn little pay and are often exposed to hazardous chemicals. They receive inadequate food, water, and shelter.

Sitting with her siblings, a five-year-old girl breaks stones at a quarry in India.

Child labor is a problem that in the past has received little attention. But people like Elizabeth Bloomer have helped raise awareness of child labor and save many children from it.

Iqbal's Story

In December 1994, a few years before Elizabeth entered Broad Meadows Middle School, the school had a special visitor—Iqbal Masih. Just twelve years old, Iqbal

13

A young girl carries a load of wool in Pakistan, where child labor laws often go unenforced.

was already gaining attention around the world by speaking out against child labor.

Iqbal was four years old when his parents sold him for two hundred dollars. They could not afford to take care of him. They thought he would have a better chance of surviving if he could work.

Iqbal was sold to a place that made carpets and rugs. He was one of many children who were chained to a floor and forced to work on a loom. His normal day of work lasted fourteen hours. Iqbal was not fed well and did not grow properly. His back curved because of lack of exercise. Each day he had to tie thousands of tiny knots, and his hands became scarred and calloused. It was hard for him to breathe because of the dust from the carpet fibers.

Finally, at age ten, Iqbal was freed by an organization called the **Bonded** Labor **Liberation** Front. This organization was founded in 1988 to fight child labor in Pakistan. It has successfully freed more than thirty thousand children from forced labor. It also operates schools.

After enduring years of grueling labor, Iqbal Masih (pictured) worked to help free other child laborers.

Iqbal's Dream

Iqbal was determined to help free other children. He traveled the world, telling his story and teaching people about child labor. He also called for a worldwide **boycott** on Pakistani-made carpets, since most were made by children. As a result, Pakistani carpet **exports** dropped between 1992 and 1994, drastically reducing the profits of the carpet industry.

For his work, Iqbal Masih received the **prestigious** Reebok Human Rights Award in 1994. This award honors young people who have made significant contributions to human rights in a nonviolent way. That same year, Broad Meadows teacher Ron Adams helped

Iqbal accepts the Reebok Human Rights award for his efforts to end child labor.

arrange for Iqbal to visit the school. It was the only school in the United States that Iqbal visited.

When the students at Broad Meadows Middle School met Iqbal and heard his story, they decided to help. They wrote nearly 670 letters to heads of state and leaders in countries where children were forced to work. The letters told Iqbal's story and voiced their opinion that child labor is wrong.

Soon after Iqbal returned home to Pakistan, he was shot and killed. It is not known who his murderers were, but many suspect that businesspeople in the carpet industry killed Iqbal in revenge for speaking out and hurting their profits.

"Can't Kill a Dream"

The news enraged the students at Broad Meadows Middle School, and they decided to take further action. They began a project called the Kids Campaign to Build a School for Iqbal. Their goal was to raise money to construct a school in the Pakistani village where Iqbal had lived. Iqbal had explained to the students that education is an important factor in stopping child labor. Like Iqbal, many children are sold into slavery because their parents need money or cannot afford to take care of them. Children who can read and write have a better chance of getting a paying job and earning money to help their families than those who cannot.

To raise money, the Broad Meadows students used their one computer with online access to contact other schools.

They shared Iqbal's story and encouraged other kids to donate money to help their efforts to stop child labor. Children throughout the United States and twenty-one countries participated. Together, they raised $143,000.

After the money was raised, the Broad Meadows students worked closely with an organization in Pakistan called Sudhaar to get the school built. The money was also used to establish the Iqbal Masih Educational Fund, which pays for the school's day-to-day activities.

Teacher Ron Adams offered guidance to Amanda Loos (center) and Elizabeth Bloomer (right), student leaders of the Kids Campaign to Build a School for Iqbal.

Students at the School for Iqbal in Pakistan salute Iqbal Masih and all those who helped open the school.

Another program that the organization created helps families buy back their children from slave labor. As a result of these accomplishments, Broad Meadows Middle School won the Reebok Human Rights award in 1995.

The School for Iqbal opened in 1997. That same year, at the age of twelve, Elizabeth Bloomer became a member of the group that had made the school a reality. She eventually became one of its lead spokespeople. She says of the group, "One of our mottos is: A bullet can't kill a dream. I thought that was horrible that someone would shoot a little boy, probably for standing up for what's right. . . . We're his voice." [6]

Elizabeth worried that after the school opened, interest in child slavery and labor would fade. She decided to continue to work to help raise awareness. Elizabeth spent about eight hours a week, after school, with her classmates. Together they tried to come up with ways they could keep on educating people about child labor. "We don't want our work to end with this one school," [7] Elizabeth says.

Chapter Three

Raising Awareness

After the School for Iqbal had been built, Elizabeth Bloomer wanted to continue the hard work her classmates had begun. Because she could not physically go to other countries and free children from child labor, she decided to use an ability she did have—a natural talent for public speaking. Elizabeth knew she had to help share the concerns she and many others had about the plight of the world's working children.

Elizabeth began to speak at every possible opportunity to educate people about child labor. She soon became the lead spokesperson at her school. She explains: "I think being in a big family helped me to become comfortable speaking in front of people and become outgoing." [8]

A Speaking Career

Her speaking career began on December 4, 1997, soon after the School for Iqbal opened.

Elizabeth was a presenter at a teachers' workshop held at the site of the historic Boott Cotton Mills in Lowell, Massachusetts. Because the mills employed many children in the early 1900s, the location was a perfect setting for Elizabeth and her classmates to speak about child labor. The students gave a speech in which they told Iqbal's story and provided facts about working children around the world.

That same fall, Elizabeth and her classmates learned about the Global March Against Child Labor, a worldwide event planned for January 1998 that asked people to walk to help raise awareness of child workers. The march was planned to take place at the same time that the United Nations International Labor Organization was meeting in Geneva, Switzerland. Members of the march wanted to pressure those attending the meeting to support new regulations that would protect children from the worst forms of child labor.

A Different Kind of March

Since most Broad Meadows students could not actually take part in the Global March, they decided to hold a different kind of walk using the Internet. Students encouraged people around the world to send them e-mail messages about child labor. Each message represented one virtual mile marched. The students collected more than three thousand messages, which they were asked to present in Washington, D.C., at a June 1998 meeting about child labor. Afterward, Elizabeth explained the goals of the online march:

Elizabeth, shown here addressing her classmates, used her talent for public speaking to tell people about child labor.

We're trying to get people informed that children are being harassed and dictated to. That's one thing the Online March does—it gives information to people that don't have a lot of knowledge. Child labor really is kind of concealed, so it's not like an open topic that's on the news every night. So we're

A young boy listens to speakers during a rally in support of the Global March Against Child Labor in 1998.

trying to get the message out that people—children—don't have a lot of rights.[9]

Operation Day's Work

Not long after delivering the e-mail messages, Elizabeth made another trip to Washington, D.C., with several classmates and teacher Ron Adams. They were there to take part in a Congressional **Roundtable** on Youth Activism. Each year, students from around the country are invited to this conference, where they speak on various issues.

The year Elizabeth attended, the nation of Haiti had recently been devastated by a hurricane. Families lost everything they had. Parents could not support their children, and many children had been sold into slavery. The focus of the meeting was on helping the people of Haiti recover.

One of the topics discussed at the meeting was starting a program called Operation Day's Work in the United States. First begun in Norway, this student-run program aims to help areas of the world in need. It also promotes leadership, activism, and community building.

When she returned to Broad Meadows Middle School, Elizabeth introduced the program to the students. They agreed to make Broad Meadows Middle one of six **pilot** schools for Operation Day's Work-USA. The other pilot schools were in Vermont, Wisconsin, North Dakota, Minnesota, and the District of Columbia.

Students in the six schools scheduled one or more days during which they worked at various jobs such as mowing lawns and washing cars. They donated the

Elizabeth and other students raised money for Haiti's hurricane victims. Many, like this woman, lost everything in the hurricane.

money they earned to the program. In total, the children who participated in Operation Day's Work raised $31,000. They also collected twenty boxes of clothes that were shipped to Haiti to aid hurricane victims. Haitian children also received livestock, seeds for planting, and money for education.

Inspired by their sister, Elizabeth's younger sisters and brother also became involved with Operation Day's Work. Mary Bloomer said, "Operation Day's Work is a great experience for kids. We are kids, helping kids to help themselves. When you help someone, it feels good. Joining [Operation Day's Work]-USA helps you to take action against things you think are not fair." [10]

Ending Child Labor

Although Elizabeth was proud of what she accomplished with Operation Day's Work, raising awareness about child labor was still the most important goal for her. One way she did this was to organize a group of students to go to the local mall on a child-labor-free shopping trip. The idea was to find clothing and other items guaranteed to have been made without child labor.

Elizabeth led the students to various stores to check product labels. The group spoke to store managers to ask if the things they sold were made by children or, at

A young boy helps his parents with the green bean harvest on a Florida farm.

clothing stores, if the cotton used to make the clothes was picked by children. The responses shocked the students. Some managers told them that the answers to these questions were none of their business and asked them to leave. Others said the cotton and clothing was child-labor-free, but could not prove it. "It really opened our eyes to how difficult it is to shop with a conscience,"[11] says Elizabeth. The group found very few products made in the United States, where child labor laws are for the most part strictly enforced.

A U.S. Problem, Too

Yet child labor is a problem in the United States, too. Elizabeth explains: "Too many children are in the fields in Texas or California or Florida or Maryland picking crops month after month, growing season after growing season, moving state to state, sprayed by insecticides, sometimes with no running water or toilets in the field. Too many spend their childhoods in the fields and not in the classrooms."[12]

Like other child advocates, Elizabeth believes that five things must happen in order to end child labor, both in the United States and elsewhere. First, all children must receive an education so they can earn money to help their families rather than being sold into slavery. Second, governments must pass and enforce strict laws against child labor. Third, companies must abide by these laws and not hire or buy children to work, or buy products made by children. Fourth, consumers should refuse to buy products that have been made by chil-

Elizabeth speaks at the United Nations in an effort to make people aware of child labor around the world.

dren. And finally, poverty must be reduced so that families can afford to support their children.

Elizabeth Speaks Out

Elizabeth explained these five factors in one of the most important speeches she has ever given. In March 2001, Elizabeth, just fifteen years old, delivered a thirty-minute speech at the United Nations to nine hundred **delegates** from around the world. Once again, her goal was to raise awareness about the problems of child labor. The speech was followed by a fifteen-minute question-and-answer session, which Elizabeth admitted made her nervous. Usually, classmates were by her side when she gave a speech, but this time, she was alone at the podium.

Despite being nervous, however, she answered questions with confidence. Her message to the United Nations was clear: "Poverty is the main cause of child exploitation. However, ending child labor is not just as simple as building schools or raising money. We have to educate people that ending child labor is very complex." [13]

Through her speeches and activism, Elizabeth Bloomer educated thousands of people about child labor. She has helped raise thousands of dollars to help children around the world. She is living proof that one person, even a young one, can make a difference.

Chapter Four

"Never Too Young"

A lthough millions of children around the world still labor in horrible conditions, people like Elizabeth Bloomer are working hard to make their lives better. Even though Elizabeth has gone on to college and a career of her own, she remains committed to helping others.

Off to College

After graduating from Archbishop Williams High School, Elizabeth was accepted to attend College of the Holy Cross in Worcester, Massachusetts. This college is well known for its educational excellence and is the oldest Catholic college in New England. Elizabeth majored in English and education. Her ultimate goal is to follow in Ron Adams's footsteps and teach at Broad Meadows Middle School.

Elizabeth enjoyed her studies at Holy Cross. Her love for running did not stop either, and she became a member of the track-and-field team. Elizabeth's faith also stayed strong at Holy Cross. She worked at the school's church, helping prepare it for Mass.

Still Helping Others

In many ways, Elizabeth was a typical college student, but in one way she was quite different from her classmates. While many of them retreated to sunny vacation spots during their spring breaks, Elizabeth used this time to help others as a member of her school's Appalachia Service Project. Students who participate in the program visit different areas of the country during spring break, volunteering their time and hard work. Services include staffing **soup kitchens**, repairing homes, and working at fire stations, homeless shelters, and schools. During freshman and sophomore years, Elizabeth went to Kentucky as a member of the project.

Elizabeth also traveled to Papua New Guinea. In June 2005, she and several other volunteers spent three and a half weeks there as part of a program called Habitat for Humanity International. This program sends ten to twelve students to a different country each year to build a house for a local family. Because only a handful of students are chosen for the program, Elizabeth had to apply to participate. She and the other volunteers were selected because of their leadership qualities, compassion, and desire to make a difference. Once Elizabeth was accepted, she had to raise forty-five hundred dollars for the trip, which she accomplished by seeking donations from friends, family members, and businesses.

Two months later, in August 2005, Hurricane Katrina destroyed many parts of New Orleans and the coast of Mississippi. Certain areas of New Orleans were completely destroyed, and in early 2006, people were still homeless. Elizabeth and other volunteers

Elizabeth Bloomer enjoys a rare moment of relaxation.

helped out in March 2006. As part of the clean-up efforts, for a week she gutted houses that had been abandoned. Once the damaged homes were demolished, new homes could be built. She says, "It was the hardest physical labor I've ever done, but it was so rewarding!" [14]

Children Helping Children

Besides helping people directly, Elizabeth Bloomer has inspired others to get involved, including her own siblings. Mary, Laura, Kristen, and Thomas have all joined the fight to end child labor and all participate in

Elizabeth poses with a young friend in Papua New Guinea, while volunteering with Habitat for Humanity.

Young activists including Laura and Mary Bloomer, Ryan Hreljac, and Elizabeth Bloomer (left to right) took part in the World Youth Congress in Scotland.

Operation Day's Work-USA. Elizabeth's other two sisters, Julie and Caroline, hope also to follow in Elizabeth's footsteps when they enter middle school. In July 2005, Elizabeth accompanied Mary and Laura to Scotland to share Iqbal's story at the World Youth Congress. This event brought six hundred young activists from 120 countries together to promote volunteering and global citizenship.

To some children, what Elizabeth and others have done seems like a lot, but their efforts all started with one thing—a passion. Elizabeth believes that she has been given certain gifts and talents, and through these, she has found her passion in life—helping children. "I had a responsibility to help others," [15] she said regarding her gifts.

A passion like Elizabeth's, however, is not always enough to enable a child to become involved. Elizabeth says, "I think that the first thing a child needs is an adult that will listen to them. When the seventh and eighth graders at Broad Meadows decided to build a school in Pakistan, they had the heart and desire to make a difference, but the fact remains that they needed the help of a trusted adult to help them be taken seriously." [16] At school, Ron Adams was that trusted adult. He believed in the vision of the students and guided them along the way. Elizabeth's family has also played a huge role in her success as an activist. Her parents continually supported her hard work and desire to help others.

Helping Those in the Community

Anyone who wants to make a difference as Elizabeth has can find many ways to help people. Churches and scouting programs are a great place to start. Many schools, too, have programs aimed at helping the community. A teacher or principal can explain what these programs are and how students can get involved.

Local charities often need help as well. Many need food, clothing, and money as well as time from volunteers. Most charities have Web sites that tell people how they can donate items. Making a difference can be a click on the computer away! Most important, anyone can help, no matter what age he or she is. The accomplishments of Elizabeth Bloomer prove it.

"Never Too Young"

Elizabeth's hard work has been rewarding in many ways. Not only has she been able to travel throughout the country and the world, she has experienced first-hand the joy of helping others. Although the battle against child labor continues, Elizabeth and her school-mates have seen many changes. The School for Iqbal in Pakistan was an important step. Today, the school continues to provide education and hope to local families.

Students volunteer for Operation Day's Work-USA, one of the many organizations created to help those in need.

Elizabeth emphasizes that even kids can take action to stop child labor abuses. "Do something to stop it," she says. "It is the right thing to do! You are never too young to take action." [17]

Elizabeth plans to continue to work with children, helping them reach their goals and dreams. In the process, she wants to show children that they can also help others. Her faith and her family keep her focused on these goals and give her the strength to continue making a difference in the lives of children all around the world.

Notes

Chapter One: Just a Regular Kid

1. Elizabeth Bloomer, e-mail message to author, December 28, 2005.
2. Quoted in *Boston Globe,* "Child's Death Stirs Another Crusade," March 2, 2001.
3. Elizabeth Bloomer, speech given at a youth retreat at Manresa at College of the Holy Cross, Worcester, MA, November 2004.

Chapter Two: "A Bullet Can't Kill a Dream"

4. Elizabeth Bloomer, e-mail message to author, February 16, 2006.
5. Bloomer, e-mail message, February 16, 2006.
6. Quoted in Student Express, "Child Slavery: A Bullet Can't Kill a Dream." www.studentxpress.ie/features/slavery.html.
7. Quoted in John Terry and Donna Woonteiler, "The Kids Online March Against Child Labor," New Designs for Youth Development. www.cydjournal.org/NewDesigns/ND_98Fall/Terry_A0.html.

Chapter Three: Raising Awareness

8. Elizabeth Bloomer, e-mail interview with author, March 13, 2006.

9. Quoted in Terry and Woonteiler, "The Kids Online March Against Child Labor."

10. Quoted in "What Kids Are Saying," Operation Day's Work. www.usaid.gov/odw.

11. Elizabeth Bloomer, e-mail message to author, June 14, 2006.

12. Quoted in Child Labor Coalition, "Message of the Month." http://stopchildlabor.org.

13. Elizabeth Bloomer, speech given to the United Nations, New York, March 2, 2001.

Chapter Four: "Never Too Young"
14. Elizabeth Bloomer, e-mail interview with author, March 27, 2006.

15. Elizabeth Bloomer, e-mail interview with author, December 28, 2005.

16. Elizabeth Bloomer, e-mail interview with author, April 18, 2006.

17. Quoted in Youth Action Net, "Elizabeth Bloomer." www.youthactionnet.org/youthprofiles/Elizabeth_1071.cfm.

Glossary

activists: People who are involved in supporting or opposing a cause.

advocate: Someone who speaks or fights on behalf of someone else.

bonded: Working in conditions similar to slavery.

boycott: To protest by not using, buying, or dealing something.

child labor: Full-time employment of children who are under legal working age.

compassion: The desire to help someone in distress.

delegates: People who represent other people or groups at a specific event.

exploitive: Taking unfair advantage of someone.

exports: Goods made in one country and shipped to other countries for sale.

graphic: Very realistic.

liberation: The act of setting someone or something free.

Mass: A Catholic church service.

pilot: Something new that is started on a trial basis.

prestigious: Held in high regard.

roundtable: A conference with several participants.

soup kitchens: Places that give food to the needy.

For Further Exploration

Books

Tanya Roberts Davis, *We Need to Go to School: Voices of the Rugmark Children*. Ontario, Canada: Groundwood, 2001. Twenty former carpet weavers give their accounts of their lives in Nepal, India, and Pakistan. The book explains how the Rugmark rug labeling program is striving to reduce child labor in this part of the world.

Russell Freedman and Lewis Hine, *Kids at Work*. New York: Clarion, 1998. Freedman describes child labor in the United States in the early twentieth century and the efforts of photographer Lewis Hine to stop it. The book includes many of Hine's photographs of children working at various jobs.

Susan Kuklin, *Iqbal Masih and the Crusaders Against Child Labor*. New York: Henry Holt, 1998. This book provides a close look at child labor overseas and tells the story of one boy's efforts to help stop child labor.

Marvin J. Levine, *Children for Hire: The Perils of Child Labor in the United States*. Westport, CT: Praeger, 2003. Levine takes a hard look at child labor in the United States from the mid-nineteenth century to the present.

Web Sites

Child Labor Coalition (www.stopchildlabor.org). The Web site of this national network informs and educates people on child labor to raise awareness and help change public policy on this issue.

End Child Labor (www.endchildlabor.org). This Web site was created to raise awareness about child labor around the world.

Global March Against Child Labor (www.global march.org). This Web site is dedicated to promoting the rights of all children and to raising awareness about abuses against children.

Operation Day's Work-USA (www.usaid.gov/odw). The official Web site for Operation Day's Work-USA, a national program run by students to help developing countries.

Rugmark (www.rugmark.org). The official Web site of Rugmark, a global nonprofit organization working to end child labor in countries such as Nepal, India, and Pakistan.

Index

Picture Credits

Cover: Courtesy of the Bloomer Family
AP/Wide World Photos, 15, 24, 26, 27
Courtesy of the Bloomer Family, 5, 9, 10, 29,
  33, 34, 35
Courtesy of Operation Day's Work, 37
Courtesy of Ron Adams, 6, 18, 19, 23
Getty Images, 14
© John Van Hasselt/CORBIS SYGMA, 16
Reuters/Landov, 13

About the Author

Jennifer Reed is an award-winning author of ten children's books, including a picture book titled *The Falling Flowers*. She is a professor of children's literature at the Institute of Children's Literature and has published over a hundred stories and articles in children's magazines. Reed lives in Maryland with her husband and two children.